The QUIZZER Bo

WEATHER

Prepared in consultation with
BRIAN P. PRICE, B.Sc., F.R.G.S.

Written and Edited by
GEORGE BEAL

Illustrated by
BRIAN PRICE-THOMAS

OWLET BOOKS

17-19 Foley Street
London

HOW WEATHER WORKS   Pages

WEATHER CONDITIONS

N T S

WEATHER FORECASTING

WEATHER RECORDS

QUIZZER BOOKS
© 1975 Hampton House Productions Limited
UK and Commonwealth edition first published by
Mills & Boon Limited
London · Toronto · Sydney

SHOW ME
THE
COLOURS
OF A
RAINBOW.

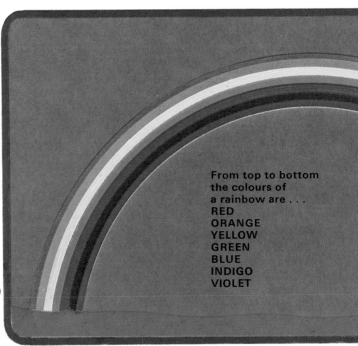

From top to bottom
the colours of
a rainbow are . . .
RED
ORANGE
YELLOW
GREEN
BLUE
INDIGO
VIOLET

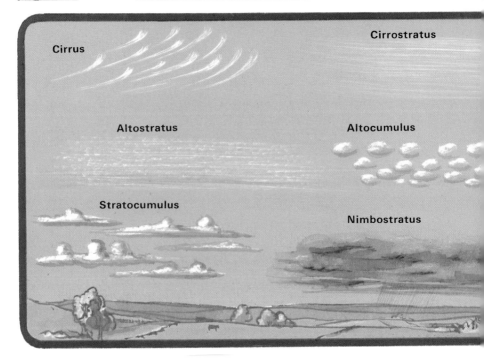

Cirrus

Cirrostratus

Altostratus

Altocumulus

Stratocumulus

Nimbostratus

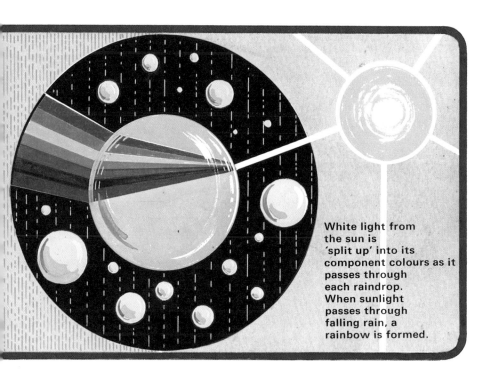

White light from the sun is 'split up' into its component colours as it passes through each raindrop. When sunlight passes through falling rain, a rainbow is formed.

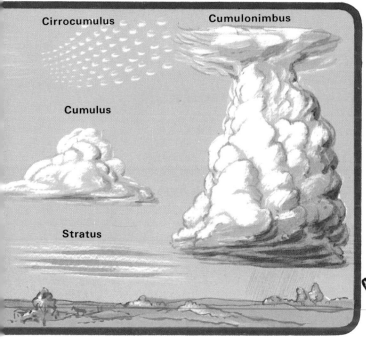

Cirrocumulus

Cumulonimbus

Cumulus

Stratus

...AND SOME DIFFERENT SORTS OF CLOUDS...

5

WHAT IS THE THING WE CALL WEATHER?

The earth is surrounded by a huge mass of air which is called *The Atmosphere.* Every day such things as the *temperature* of this air, the amount of *moisture* in it, the speed and direction of the *wind* and the amount and type of *clouds* will be different. It is these things which add up to make *the weather.*

WHAT IS CLIMATE?

Over a period of time, perhaps as little as a month, or as long as a century, observers keep records of the weather conditions of a country or region. They measure the amount of sunshine and rainfall, the air pressure and wind speed and direction and other elements of the weather. They then say that the *average weather* of that place is its *climate.*

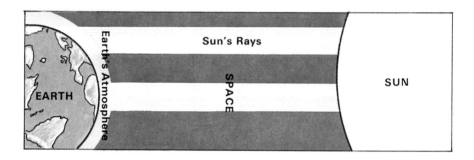

WHAT DOES THE SUN DO?

The Sun is a giant mass of burning gas a long way out in space which gives the earth *light* and *heat*. Without it, the Earth would be dark and would freeze over. Only a tiny fraction of all the Sun's energy reaches us, and about a third of the radiation which is directed at the Earth is reflected back into space by the clouds and our atmosphere before it reaches the surface.
The Sun's energy which does reach the Earth evaporates the water in the seas, lakes and rivers, which later falls as rain; it also warms the air in the atmosphere. Plants and animals need the light and warmth of the sun to live.

WHAT DO WE MEAN BY AIR PRESSURE?

Although we cannot see it, we can *feel* air. We talk of cool breezes, hot blasts, or raging gales, and all are the result of moving air. Air has *weight,* too, and is quite heavy. The air in an average-size house weighs about half a ton, although the weight of air is not always the same. Hot air in a given room of the house weighs less than cold air in the same room. When air is cold, it packs together more closely, and so weighs more.

Above every square foot of the Earth's surface there is a column of air which weighs about one ton. Because it presses down, we call this weight of air the *air pressure.* The air pressure changes slightly from day to day and is a very important element in the weather.

WHAT IS HUMIDITY?

Humidity simply means the amount of *moisture* in the air. This moisture may be in the form of a *gas, droplet* or *ice crystal.* The amount present in the air varies a good deal. When there is very little moisture in the air it feels dry, but when there is much more the air feels sticky. Humidity is an important element in the weather. Weather forecasters need to be able to measure it very accurately.

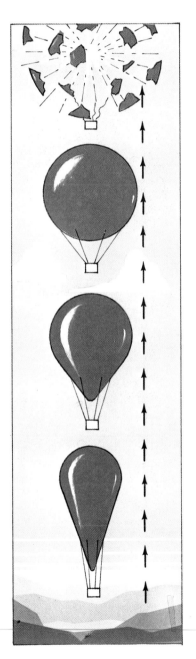

The gas inside a balloon has a pressure roughly equal to the pressure of air at ground level. As the balloon rises, the air pressure lessens. The balloon grows bigger, and eventually bursts.

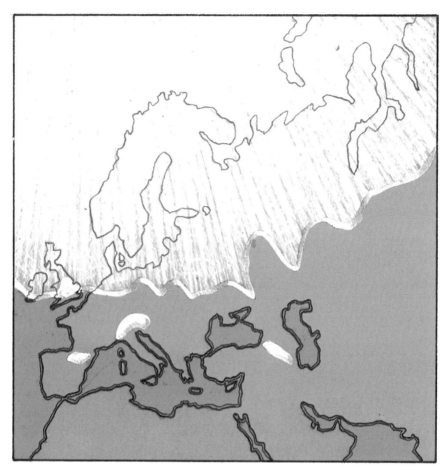

This map shows the area of Europe covered by ice as recently as 10,000 years ago. Today, only a small area around the North Pole is ice-covered.

WHEN WAS THE LAST ICE AGE?

The most recent Ice Age is still with us. The Earth has been in existence for about 5,000,000,000 years. During most of this time, the whole planet has been quite warm, with higher temperatures at the Equator than in the Polar regions.

There have been *three ice ages* during the past 1,000,000,000 years. The first was about 800,000,000 years ago, the second about 300,000,000 years ago, and the last, which began about a million years ago is still in existence. In each, sheets of ice spread over large parts of the earth's surface. As recently as 10,000 years ago most of the British Isles were covered by ice.

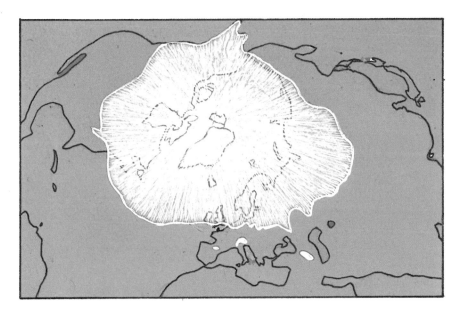

Total area of the Northern Hemisphere once covered by ice is shown on this map. The small area in the centre shows the extent of the present ice-cap.

HOW HAS THE WEATHER CHANGED THROUGH THE AGES?

Only ten centuries ago, the world was colder than it is today. It then started to become warmer, and reached a temperature peak about 6,000 years ago. Some of the ice at the north and south poles melted. The weather then became colder until shortly before Christ was alive, and then it became warmer until about 800 years ago. At that time, the weather of the temperate zone was so good that the Vikings were able to colonise Iceland and Greenland. They raised sheep and cattle on the grasslands, and grapes grew in Newfoundland, which is why the Vikings named it Vinland. Such things could not be done today.

Once more it grew cold, and the period from 1550 to 1700 has been called the *little Ice Age*. Gradually since then, the weather has become warmer, although as we know from quite recent records, winters were colder during the 19th century. Until about 1940, the temperatures rose and less rain fell. It seems that this short warm period has now come to an end, for temperatures have been lower since the 1940's. We are unlikely to enjoy summers in Britain as warm as those which our grandparents talk about.

9

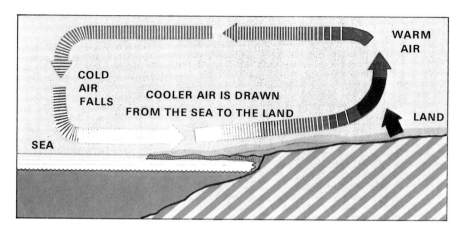

A sea breeze: diagram showing how one type of wind is formed.

WHERE DO WINDS COME FROM?

It has been said that a wind is *air in a hurry*. In fact, a wind is a movement of air caused by *differences in temperature and pressure.* Some winds are found in a small area, whilst others blow over large areas. When air is warmed, it rises; when it cools, it falls.

A radiator in a house will warm the air beside it. This air rises and other air moves in to replace it. The new air is almost always cooler, being sucked in under doors or down chimneys. The rising hot air has created a draught, which is a kind of small wind.

Similar things happen in the open air. Winds begin when the sun heats various objects or areas, since not everything gets hot at the same rate. An asphalt road, exposed to the blazing sun, will heat up more quickly than a river nearby. When the road is hot, the air above it will be heated and will rise. Cool air over the river will flow in to replace the rising hot air, and so will produce a cool breeze.

Similarly, on a sunny day, land areas heat up more quickly than the sea, with the result that cool air is drawn in on to the land as wind. As the air on the sea surface flows on to the land, even cooler air from above falls, and in its turn, is drawn to the land as wind. So we have a *circular movement* of air, which is called a *sea breeze.* At night time, when the land cools down more quickly than the sea, a *land breeze* blowing the opposite way may begin.

WHY DOES AIR PRESSURE CHANGE?

Air pressure does not stay the same at any one place for very long. The actual amount of air which is pressing down on the ground changes slightly from hour to hour because the whole mass of air in the atmosphere is always moving.
These changes are so slight that you cannot tell the differences without very special instruments called *barometers.* When there is more air pressing down we say that pressure is *high*, and when there is less we say it is *low.* Air pressure is always greater at sea level than it is on a mountain or up in an aeroplane. This is because there is less air pressing down at a height of, say 20,000 ft. than there is at sea level.

WHY DOES THE WIND CHANGE DIRECTION?

If everything on the Earth grew hot at the same rate, air would simply rise as it was heated from the warm surfaces, and fall as soon as it cooled. But the Earth is hotter at the Equator than it is at the poles. This means that on average, the air in the polar regions is colder and its pressure is higher than it is at the Equator. We also know that in summer, land areas become hotter than the seas and oceans. This means that on average, the air over the land is hotter and its pressure lower than that of air over water.
At ground level, air moves from places where the pressure is higher to those where it is lower. Some air moves away from the Poles towards the Equator; in summer other air moves away from the oceans towards the land, and in winter in the reverse directions. The shapes of the land masses and the differences in the amounts of heat received at the earth's surface lead to a very complicated pattern of winds every day of the year. Another influence on the winds is the rotation of the earth. Winds seem to be deflected by the movement of the earth beneath them.

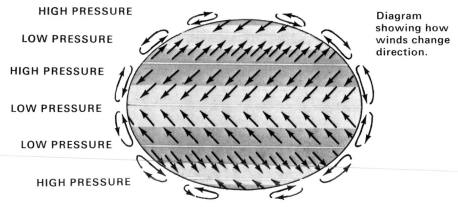

HIGH PRESSURE

LOW PRESSURE

HIGH PRESSURE

LOW PRESSURE

LOW PRESSURE

HIGH PRESSURE

Diagram showing how winds change direction.

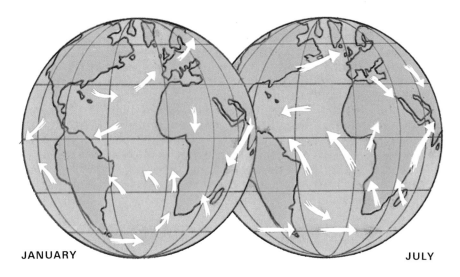

JANUARY   JULY

The arrows show the direction of prevailing winds in January and July. Trade Winds blow in the same direction throughout the year, but monsoons vary with seasons.

WHAT ARE PREVAILING WINDS?

These are the type of winds which blow in a similar direction for most of the time, or for long periods of time. The *Trade Winds,* for instance, blow in a similar direction all the year, but the *monsoons* vary at different seasons. For example, the Indian Monsoon blows from the south-west between April and June, and from the north-east in January. In the southern hemisphere, there are strong winds which blow quite regularly from the west and north-west across the great expanses of the South Atlantic, Indian and South Pacific Oceans. These are called the *Roaring Forties.* Prevailing winds were very important to seamen in the days of sailing ships.

WHERE IS WATER FOUND IN THE ATMOSPHERE?

Water can be found in three forms—*ice* (frozen form), *water* (liquid form), or *water vapour* (a gas). Heat is needed to turn ice into a liquid and a liquid into a vapour. If heat is lost, then the vapour can turn back into a liquid and eventually a solid.

All open water, whether it be ocean, river, lake, pond or a puddle, can be evaporated by the heat of the Sun. The water vapour is then absorbed into the air. At other times water vapour, or water droplets in the atmosphere, may return to the earth's surface as rain, snow, dew or frost.

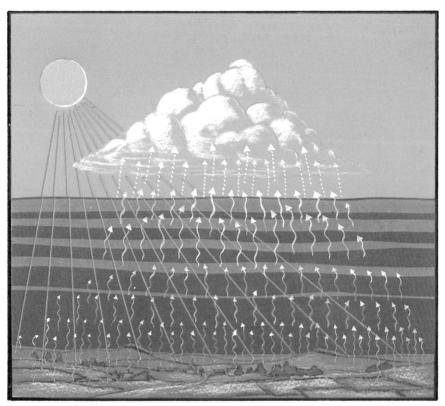

Clouds are formed after the sun turns water into water vapour. Condensed vapour forms water droplets, and these go to form clouds.

HOW ARE CLOUDS FORMED?

Every minute of the day, the heat of the sun turns a lot of water into water vapour. This vapour is absorbed into the atmosphere and may stay there for many hours or days. If the amount of vapour in the air increases beyond a certain amount, or if the air is cooled, the *water-vapour* condenses into droplets of water. These are very tiny and are called *cloud droplets*. Millions of them together form a white floating mass which we call a *cloud.*

Clouds are classified according to their height and type, using the names *cirrus,* meaning *curly; cumulus,* a *heap; stratus,* a *layer;* and *nimbus,* a *rainstorm.* Above 20,000 feet, the three types are *Cirrus, Cirro-cumulus* and *Cirro-stratus;* between 6,500 to 20,000 feet there are *Alto-cumulus* and *Alto-stratus* clouds ; and below that are *Strato-cumulus, Stratus, Nimbo-stratus*, and *Cumulus* clouds. *Cumulo-nimbus* clouds, which bring thunder and lightning, often reach from low levels right up to 30,000 feet.

13

Water vapour condenses into cloud droplets, and so forms a cloud. Rain falls when droplets become large enough.

WHY DOES IT RAIN?

Cloud droplets are so tiny that they seem to float in the air. It may take more than a million of them to join together before a droplet of water large enough, and heavy enough to fall to the ground, is made. Some rain drops are formed by the collision of cloud droplets moving about inside clouds. Others are formed when the air in the cloud is so cold that ice crystals form. These may fall through the cloud but melt into a raindrop in the warmer air nearer to the ground.

Of course, not all that falls from clouds is rain. We can also get snow, sleet and hail. These, together with frost and dew, are called *precipitation*.

When air streams rise over mountains, the air cools, and forms ice crystals. These fall, but melt into rain nearer the ground.

Cold air, moving forward, pushes warm air upwards, forming clouds, which then produce rain.

WHAT ARE THE DOLDRUMS?

The *doldrums* is the name of *a region in the tropics* where the winds are very light for weeks at a time. In the days of sailing ships, vessels were held up in the doldrums for long periods, because there was no wind to fill the sails. The region lies on both sides of the Equator, between the two belts of trade winds.

Its exact position varies from month to month, being further north in June than it is in December. The climate of the doldrums is hot and humid, with cloudy skies, very light variable winds, many thunderstorms, calms and squalls.

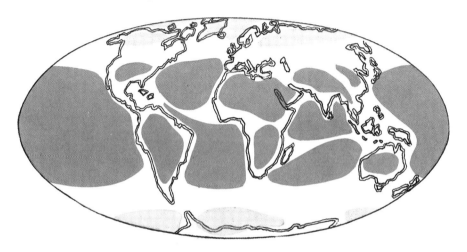

Air masses are known as *maritime* if formed over oceans, and *continental* if formed over land.

WHAT ARE AIR MASSES AND AIR STREAMS?

When a large amount of air in one place has similar humidity and temperature, it is called an *air mass.* Air masses are formed over some parts of the world, which are called *air mass source regions.* Arctic and Antarctic air masses are formed near the North and South Poles and Equatorial air masses are formed in the tropics. Polar air masses have their source area about one third of the way from the polar to the equator; tropical air masses have their source area about one third of the way from the equator to the poles. Air masses are known as *Maritime* if they have formed over the oceans, and *Continental,* if they have formed over land. So we can have Maritime Polar or Continental Tropical air masses, and so on. Once an air mass moves away from its source area it is called an *air stream.*

WHAT ARE POLAR FRONTS?

When one air stream meets another air stream the properties of one are often different from the other. In the atmosphere, *the zone in which the two air streams meet* is called a front. The zone where Polar air meets Tropical air is known as a *Polar Front.* The main ones are found over the Northern Atlantic Ocean and the North Pacific Ocean, roughly between the latitudes of 40° and 60°. There are others in the South Atlantic, South Pacific and Indian Oceans. The weather near to a polar front changes a lot from day to day, as it does in Britain.

WHAT ARE WARM FRONTS AND COLD FRONTS?

If one air stream is warm—as with a Tropical one—and the other is cold—as with a Polar one—then we speak of a warm or cold front, depending on which way the front is moving.
A *warm front* occurs when warm air follows cold. The warm air moves up to and rides over the cold air. When cold air follows warm, the cold air slides under the warm air, and this produces a *cold front.* Both warm and cold fronts often bring rainy weather.

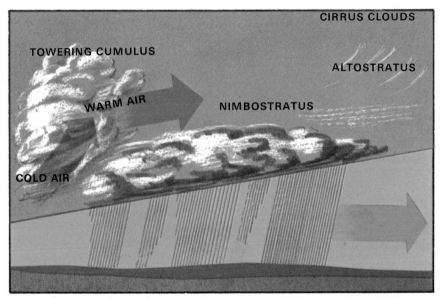

In a warm front, the warm air moves up and rides over the cold air.

16

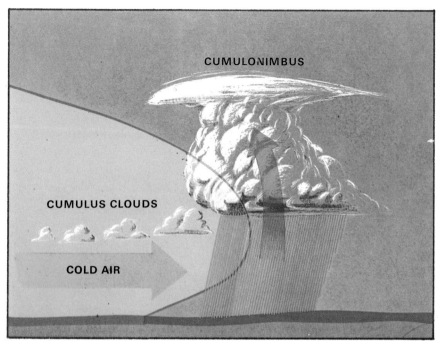

CUMULONIMBUS

CUMULUS CLOUDS

COLD AIR

When cold air follows warm, the cold air slides under the warm air, so producing a cold front.

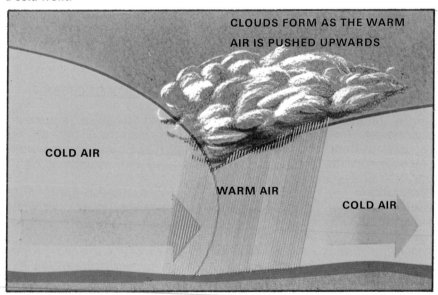

CLOUDS FORM AS THE WARM
AIR IS PUSHED UPWARDS

COLD AIR

WARM AIR

COLD AIR

If a cold front overtakes a warm front, the cold air meets more cold, causing the warm air to be lifted, and this is called an occlusion. Usually, this causes heavy rain.

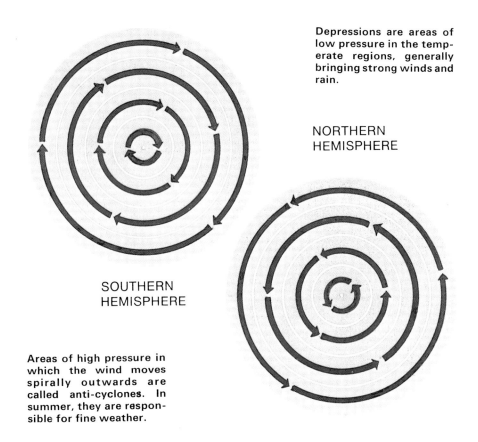

Depressions are areas of low pressure in the temperate regions, generally bringing strong winds and rain.

NORTHERN HEMISPHERE

SOUTHERN HEMISPHERE

Areas of high pressure in which the wind moves spirally outwards are called anti-cyclones. In summer, they are responsible for fine weather.

WHAT ARE DEPRESSIONS AND ANTI-CYCLONES?

In the temperate regions, *an area of low pressure* is called a *depression.* The word cyclone is used to describe a tropical low pressure system. In a depression, the air moves spirally inwards— clockwise in the southern hemisphere and anti-clockwise in the northern hemisphere.

Depressions are generally bad-weather systems, bringing strong winds and lots of rain. A depression covers a large area, often about a thousand miles across. A deep depression is one with very low pressure at its centre.

An *anticyclone* is *an area of high pressure* in which the wind moves spirally outwards; clockwise in the northern hemisphere and anti-clockwise in the southern hemisphere. In summer, an anticyclone is responsible for fine weather, but in winter, some will bring clear skies and cold weather and others bring cloudy skies.

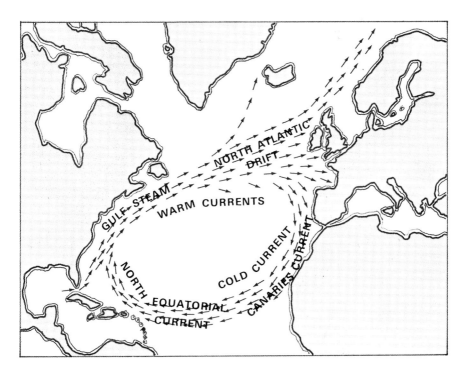

Map showing the ocean currents of the Atlantic

HOW DO OCEAN CURRENTS AFFECT THE WEATHER?

In the oceans of the world, currents of warm water move for thousands of miles from one area to another. In other places currents of cold water move over similar distances. Where a warm current flows past a land area it may help to make the weather milder than it would otherwise be. A cold current flowing past a land area may help to make the weather cooler.

One example of an ocean current is found in the North Atlantic Ocean. Warm water flows from the Caribbean Sea north-eastwards along the east coast of the United States, and then across to the west coast of Europe, including the British Isles. This stream of warm water helps to keep the seas around the coasts of Iceland, Norway and northern Russia free of ice during the winter, and the temperatures higher than might be expected. The Gulf Stream forms part of the North Atlantic current.

SHOW ME HOW THE WEATHER WORKS . . .

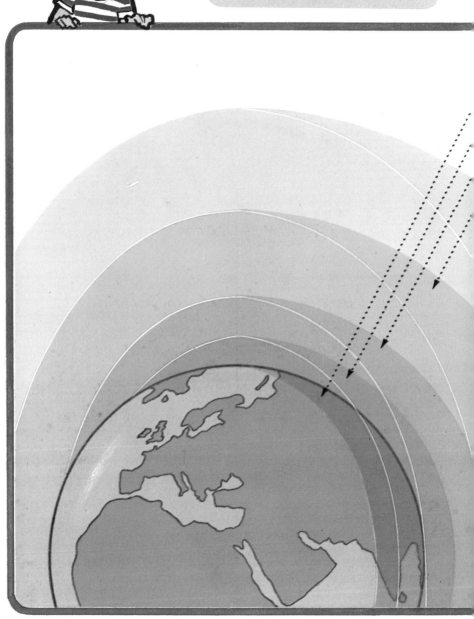

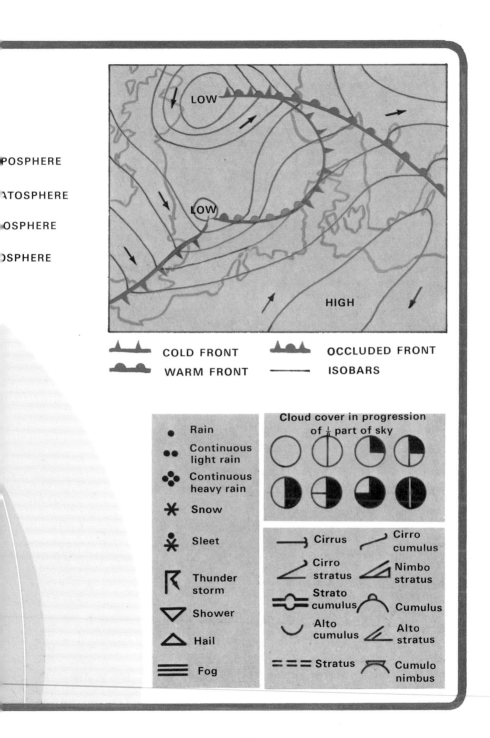

POSPHERE

ATOSPHERE

OSPHERE

OSPHERE

LOW

LOW

HIGH

COLD FRONT   OCCLUDED FRONT

WARM FRONT   ISOBARS

- Rain
•• Continuous light rain
•:• Continuous heavy rain
✳ Snow
✴ Sleet
⌐ Thunder storm
▽ Shower
△ Hail
≡ Fog

Cloud cover in progression of ⅛ part of sky

Cirrus   Cirro cumulus
Cirro stratus   Nimbo stratus
Strato cumulus   Cumulus
Alto cumulus   Alto stratus
Stratus   Cumulo nimbus

Ice, forming in a cloud, may break up into many tiny crystals, which may cling together, forming a snowflake.

WHY DOES IT SNOW?

Snow is formed in a similar way to raindrops, except that the temperature is lower. As we know, clouds consist of water vapour which has condensed. When the air temperature in the cloud is above freezing point, cloud droplets are formed. When the temperature is below freezing point, ice crystals are formed. When these ice crystals become too large to stay in the cloud, they may reach the ground as a solid mass of ice, called a *hailstone*, or they may break up into lots of tiny ice crystals, many of which cling together to make a *snowflake*.

Snow can only fall when the temperature in the cloud is below freezing point, though it can reach the ground when the temperature there is just above freezing point.

WHAT IS A SNOWFLAKE?

When water freezes, it forms itself into tiny ice crystals, and each one of these is *hexagonal-shaped*—that is, it is a shape, or figure, with six sides. This can be seen by examining a snowflake under a microscope. A snowflake is made up of a number of these crystals joined together. Snowflakes are formed when the temperature is not too low, and the ice-crystals can stick together. In extremely cold weather, the ice-crystals remain separate and do not form snowflakes.

When snow falls, each snowflake will be regular in shape. Snowflakes are more or less star-shaped, each with an icy centre. From this centre, tiny rods of ice project all round, like sunrays. From these rays other, even smaller rays or spikes project, so that the overall effect is a very beautiful star-shape. The patterns made by snowflakes are of tremendous variety, but all are six-sided, based on the shape of each crystal.

SHOW ME SOME DIFFERENT SORTS OF SNOW— FLAKES . . .

Ice crystals are hexago-nal-shaped. This means that they are formed into a figure with six sides. Based on this six-sided figure, snowflakes form a huge variety of beauti-fully-shaped patterns, some of which are shown here.

WHAT ARE MIST AND FOG?

If a glass is filled with ice, and allow it to stand in a warm room, tiny drops of water will form on the outside of the glass. This is because the air around the glass contains moisture in the form of water-vapour, the ice cools the actual glass and the water vapour condenses on the cold surface. The same thing will happen on windows. If the room is warm and the windows cold, then you will often find that the windows mist-up with tiny droplets of water.
All air contains water vapour, and it only requires a fall in temperature for it to condense into water. Clouds are simply masses of very tiny droplets of water, and a mist and fog is made in a similar way. You can think of mist and fog as cloud sitting on the ground. In the case of mist and fog, dirt and dust in the atmosphere result in a thicker, often more persistent cloud. The water vapour condenses on the particles of dust. A weather man says that there is mist when you can see no further than 2,000 yards, and that there is fog when you can see no further than 1,000 yards. In dense fog, visibility may be as low as a few yards.

WHAT ARE HAILSTONES?

A hailstone is *a mass of ice* which falls from a cloud during a storm. If we split open a hailstone, we can see that it contains a central core of ice, surrounded by a number of layers of ice, rather as an onion is made up of layers. This gives us a clue as to how they are formed. We know that when it is warm rain falls from clouds. If the temperature is low enough, then snow falls. Sometimes, too, what starts falling as snow melts and falls as rain.
Hailstones are not, as is sometimes thought, simply frozen drops of rain. Inside some very large clouds, which may be towering cumulus or cumulo-nimbus, there are strong up-currents. Tiny droplets of water are carried up on these until they reach levels when the temperature is below freezing. There the water freezes into a tiny ice crystal. Eventually the up-current of air stops, and the ice crystal falls back through the cloud. As it does this it may collide with other droplets of water which then freeze to it. In this way the size of the ice mass grows. Often the ice will be carried up through the cloud and drop back a number of times before it finally falls to the ground as a hailstone. It can be said that the larger the hailstone, the more times it has been up and down inside the cloud.

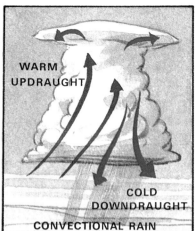

A cumulonimbus cloud. The red arrows show the warm, moist air rising, and the blue arrows the cold downdraught.

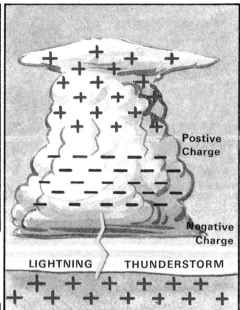

This picture shows the top of the cloud and the earth with positive electrical charges, and the lower part of the cloud negatively charged. Lightning occurs when a flash jumps from the top to the bottom of the cloud, or from the cloud to the earth.

HAILSTONES, FORMED
AND BUILT IN CLOUD

This is an enlarged view of a cut-open hailstone, to show the onion-like structure of the various layers.

The pictures on this page show how thunder and lightning are caused, and how hailstones are formed. The picture at bottom left shows how droplets of water are carried up into the cloud. These droplets freeze into small ice crystals which later fall back, colliding with other ice crystals, which together form the hailstone.

WHAT IS LIGHTNING?

Thunder and lightning are heard and seen during a thunderstorm. All thunderstorms take place in *cumulonimbus clouds* — the tall clouds which stretch up to 30,000 ft., and sometimes higher. As with any sort of rain, the falling drops of water in a storm fall towards the earth, but sometimes a rising column of air comes up to meet them. This breaks up the raindrops, and at the same time, the breaking-up action gives them an electric charge. Some places in the cloud build up a strong positive charge and other places build up a strong negative charge. The earth itself can act as a centre with a positive charge as well.

Eventually the build-up of electricity becomes so strong that the current flashes across the hot air, and this flash is what we see as lightning. Lightning can occur inside one cloud, between one cloud and another, or between a cloud and the earth beneath it.

WHY DOES IT THUNDER?

Thunder and lightning are both produced at the same time. We see the lightning flash first, because light travels very much faster than sound.

The sound of thunder is produced at the same time as a stroke of lightning, and is part of the same event. Lightning produces enormous heat, sometimes as much as 45,000 °C (80,000°F). This heat causes the air to expand violently. Pressure or shock waves travel in all directions. Some reach the human ear, and are heard as a loud bang or series of bangs and cracks.

Light travels very fast, but sound waves travel much more slowly. It is for this reason, that we hear the sound of thunder after we have seen the lightning. The interval between the flash and the sound varies depending on how far away it occurred. Since the light reaches your eyes at about the same moment as the electrical discharge takes place, but sound takes about five seconds to travel one mile, you can count the time difference between the flash and the bang, divide by five and say how many miles away the thunderstorm is.

Although deserts are dry places, some rain does fall occasionally. Most deserts are on the west of continents, or in the centre of land areas. Winds that blow are dry, producing very little rain.

WHAT IS A DESERT?

A desert is a large area of land where very little rain falls, and where very few plants grow. Apart from the *ice-deserts* in the polar regions, the world's deserts are situated in the tropical areas. Most of them are on the west side of a continent, or in the centre of a large land mass. None is on the east side of a continent. The trade winds blow over the desert areas of the world, blowing from land to the sea. The air in these winds is very dry, and hence very little rain falls. Although deserts are hot and dry, it is wrong to think that the temperature is always high—it often is during the day, but at night it drops very quickly and it can be very cold.

Deserts are not completely dry, as a little rain does fall occasionally. There are also oases in deserts, and these are found where rocks, which hold water, reach the surface of the desert. There are some rivers which bring water to deserts and support life in them. The River Nile flows right across the Sahara Desert and the River Colorado flows right across the deserts in the south-west U.S.A.

TELL ME ABOUT JUNGLES!

Jungles are found in South America, Africa and parts of South East Asia, near to the equator. The wet, hot climate allows a tremendous amount of tropical vegetable life to grow. These are the parts of the world where the total rainfall is the heaviest. The heavier the rainfall, the denser the jungle. In these equatorial regions, rain falls on most days of the year, and is combined with intervals of very hot sunshine.

WHAT IS FROST?

The *white dust of ice crystals* seen on our gardens on many winter mornings is frost. It is formed when the Earth loses its heat, and when the dew point is below freezing point. The water vapour in the air condenses, and immediately becomes ice in the form of tiny crystals. Freezing begins at ground level, known as *ground frost*, and later this spreads into the air above, when it is called an *air frost*. It is most usual for frost to form when the sky is clear and when the air is still. Just as we have seen that the inside of your windows can mist up with water droplets on a cold night, on a very cold night the glass may become so cold that the water freezes to the inside of the window forming a pretty pattern.

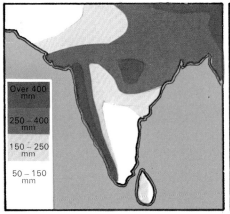 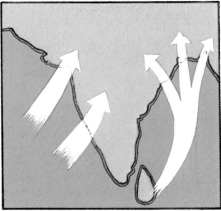

Over 400 mm

250 – 400 mm

150 – 250 mm

50 – 150 mm

The map on the left shows the rainfall during the July monsoon of the Indian sub-continent, and the one on the right shows the path of this monsoon.

WHAT IS A MONSOON?

The word monsoon comes from *an Arabic word meaning season.* The most famous example of a monsoon refers to winds which blow across the Indian sub-continent at certain times of the year. The monsoon between December and May is dry. Then the winds come south from Siberia and over the Himalayas. The monsoon between late May and November on the other hand, comes from the south, having passed over the Indian Ocean. It is therefore moist and warm, and brings heavy rain with it.

Other parts of the world where monsoons are found are Northern Australia and the islands of Indonesia, South-East China and the extreme eastern parts of central Africa.

Hurricanes move along at speeds of about 12 mph, but the wind in the spiral may be as great as 200 mph.

WHAT ARE HURRICANES, CYCLONES AND TYPHOONS?

A hurricane is *a powerful tropical storm* in which the wind speeds may be as great as 200 m.p.h. It is a kind of cyclone, which is an area of low pressure, around which the air spirals inwards. Hurricanes form over warm seas north and south of the equator, and are several hundred miles across. Warm moist air rises from the sea, and is forced up higher, to be replaced by cooler air which blows spirally inward around a core. Atlantic hurricanes move across the ocean and land at a speed of about 12 m.p.h. which increases as they move away from tropical waters and towards the north. A hurricane causes great damage when it reaches land areas. In Asia, hurricanes are known as *typhoons* and *cyclones*, while the Philippine name is *baguio,* and the Australian word *willy-willy.*
Probably the worst cyclone on record was that in Bangla Desh in 1970, when 1,000,000 people died in the floods and destruction caused by the heavy rain and high winds. In the United States, particularly, hurricanes created more havoc than any other single natural cause. Hurricane 'Betsy' of 1965, cost $1,000,000,000. Tropical hurricanes do not reach the British Isles, but high winds of a similar type are known. In 1953, tremendous gales, with winds of over 100 m.p.h. hit the east coast of England and Scotland, causing much damage and loss of life.

The picture above shows a tornado, a tropical storm which creates havoc in its wake. Over 600 of these occur every year in the United States alone.

Below is a waterspout. This is a tornado which travels across the sea, lifting water into its whirling centre.

WHAT DO YOU KNOW ABOUT TORNADOES?

A tornado is the most violent and destructive of all cyclones, or tropical storms. They happen in many tropical and sub-tropical regions of the world, but are most common in North America, the West Indies and Australia. Over 600 occur every year in the United States alone. Tornadoes cover a smaller area than hurricanes or cyclones, and can be as little as a few feet across. Tornadoes can be seen quite clearly as a dark-coloured, funnel-shaped column which seems to be snaking upwards from the ground like a giant spinning top. In common with all cyclones, the winds in tornadoes rotate in an anti-clockwise direction in the northern hemisphere and a clockwise direction in the southern hemisphere.

They travel across the ground at speeds of 20–30 m.p.h. and sometimes as fast as 60 m.p.h. The winds rushing around the tornado may be as strong as 300 m.p.h. Most tornadoes last for only a short while. They travel for distances of only fifty miles or so, tearing up and destroying everything in their path. A *waterspout* is a tornado which occurs over the sea, and lifts water into its *funnel.*

WHY DO WE SEE RAINBOWS?

All white light is made up of many colours. When the sun shines through clear air, its light appears to be white. When the sun shines through rain, the white light is broken up into a number of colours—red, orange, yellow, green, blue, indigo and violet. What happens is that the sunlight enters each droplet of water and is bent, or refracted, before it comes out again at some other point. When white light is refracted, each of the colours contained in it are turned at a slightly different angle, so that the eye sees these different colours spread out in a band.
It is this display of seven colours spread out in a long curved strip across the sky which we call a *rainbow*. Although several people may see a rainbow at the same time, no two people see exactly the same one, because the colours reaching each eye are being reflected at a slightly different angle.

WHY DO FLOODS HAPPEN?

Floods usually occur when rivers overflow their banks and the water spreads over the adjoining land, or when the sea breaks through coastal defences and invades low-lying land behind them. Nearly all floods in inland districts are caused by rain which swells the normal flow of rivers until they overflow. Sometimes during a freak storm more water falls in a place than can soak into the ground or flow away in the streams and rivers. Most rivers overflow their banks at some time during each year, but in recent times man has built up river banks where such floods would be disastrous, as in the centre of big towns and cities.
When ice and snow on mountains melts in the spring, the amount of water released increases quickly and floods often take place in the valleys further along the rivers.
Sea floods often occur at times of high tide and stormy weather. The sea rises, and this, combined with storms, can result in the low-lying land near coasts to be flooded over wide areas.

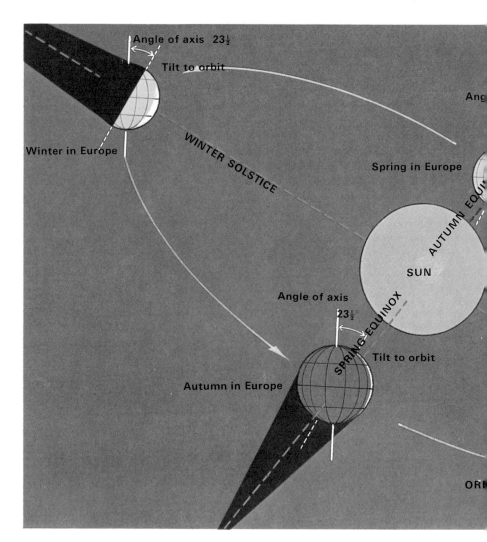

Angle of axis 23½°

Tilt to orbit

Ang

Winter in Europe

WINTER SOLSTICE

Spring in Europe

SUN

AUTUMN EQU

Angle of axis 23½°

Tilt to orbit

SPRING EQUINOX

Autumn in Europe

ORE

WHY DOES WEATHER . . .

First we have to know why the seasons occur. The Earth revolves around the sun in an orbit, and one complete revolution lasts a year. The Earth is also rotating on an axis, which is not absolutely upright. It is tilted at an angle of $23\frac{1}{2}°$ from a line drawn vertically to the plane of its path around the sun. This means that at some periods of the year, the northern hemisphere is leaning towards the Sun, and the southern hemisphere is leaning away. At other periods, the reverse is the case. When the part of the globe containing Europe is tilted away from the sun, the sun's rays reach

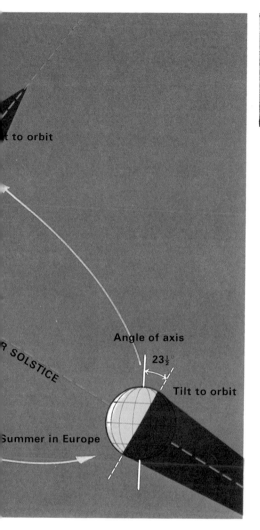

to orbit

Angle of axis

23½°

Tilt to orbit

R SOLSTICE

Summer in Europe

Only about one-sixth of an iceberg is visible above water.

DOES THE SEA EVER BECOME FROZEN?

The sea freezes in some parts of Europe each year, such as in the Baltic Sea. In North America the Great Lakes are frozen for five months every winter and all shipping stops. Other seas, like those at the North Pole and surrounding Antarctica, are frozen all the time. The fields of ice at the poles are sometimes as much as a mile thick. During the summer the ice begins to melt. Huge sections of the icefield break away and float towards the equator, and on reaching warmer seas, they break up into smaller pieces. Even these pieces are huge, and are the icebergs which are such a danger to shipping, especially in the North Atlantic.

... CHANGE WITH THE SEASONS?

Europe from a point low in the sky and have to pass through a greater part of the atmosphere than at other times. The hours of daylight are fairly short and so we have winter. When the Earth is tilted the other way the sun's rays reach Europe from a point high in the sky and have to pass through a lesser part of the atmosphere than at other times. The hours of daylight are much longer and so we have summer. When the northorn hemisphere has summer, the southern has its winter and vice-versa.

WHAT IS MEANT BY THE SCIENCE OF METEOROLOGY?

Meteorology is the study of the atmosphere. *It is the science of the weather,* and involves the measuring of what is happening, and forecasting what may happen in the future. Experts in meteorology are called *meteorologists.* They study such things as changes in temperature, air pressure, moisture in the atmosphere, the chemical state of the air, and movements of the air.

WHO INVENTED METEOROLOGY?

Men have studied the weather and climate since the dawn of history. The science of meteorology was not invented by one man, but was the result of the work of many. The first man to write on the subject was *Aristotle* in the 4th century B.C. Later work was done by such men as *Leonardo da Vinci*—who in 1500 made a wind vane—*Galileo,* who made a thermometer in about 1593, and *Torricelli,* who made a barometer in 1643. *Edmund Halley,* the astronomer and mathematician, produced an account of trade winds and monsoons in 1686, while the first weather map was drawn in 1820 by *Heinrich Wilhelm Brandes.* In 1840, *William C. Redfield* described the cyclone, recognising it as a revolving storm, and *William Ferrel* introduced the theory of the circulating atmosphere in 1856. Weather forecasting, or weather prediction, was founded in the middle 18th century by the French scientist *Jean Baptiste de Monet.*

HOW MANY YEARS HAVE WEATHER RECORDS BEEN KEPT?

The earliest surviving daily records of local weather conditions are those kept by *William Merle,* the rector of Driby, for the years 1331-1338. Almost certainly similar ones were kept but they are now lost. In 1653, *Ferdinand of Tuscany* organised a system of local stations and daily records for Northern Italy, and other records were kept near Florence from 1655-1670. A chain of meteorological stations were set up in France in the early 19th century, and the first telegraphic weather report appeared in the *Daily News* in 1848.
Although private weather records were kept for many years earlier, the Meteorological Office in Britain was opened in 1855, since which date, official records have been kept.

HOW DOES A MERCURY BAROMETER WORK?

There are several kinds of barometer, but each is used to do one sort of job, which is to measure the pressure of the atmosphere. One kind is the mercury barometer, which consists of a glass tube about 33 inches long. This tube is closed at the top end, and open at the bottom end. The tube contains mercury. The open end may either be turned around in a 'U' shape, or may rest in a reservoir of mercury. The pressure of the air pushes down on the mercury at the open end, and supports the column of mercury reaching up the tube to a height of about 30 inches. As the air pressure changes, so mercury falls and rises by a small amount.

Most mercury barometers are read by a very accurate scale which has a mirror and a fine adjusting screw. Using this, it is possible to read the height of the column of mercury to one-thousandth part of an inch.

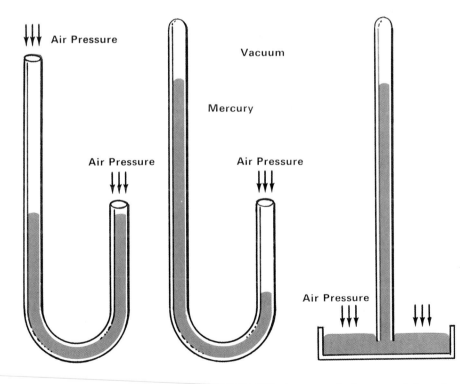

Mercury thermometers may be formed into a U-shape, or the bottom of the tube may rest in a reservoir of mercury.

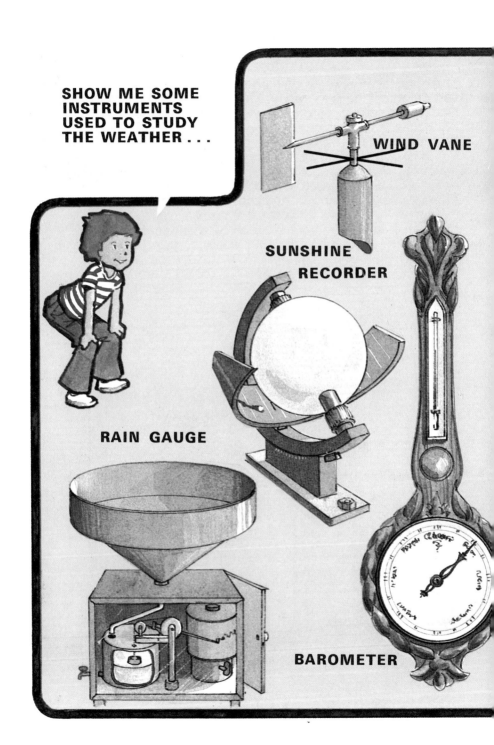

SHOW ME SOME INSTRUMENTS USED TO STUDY THE WEATHER . . .

WIND VANE

SUNSHINE RECORDER

RAIN GAUGE

BAROMETER

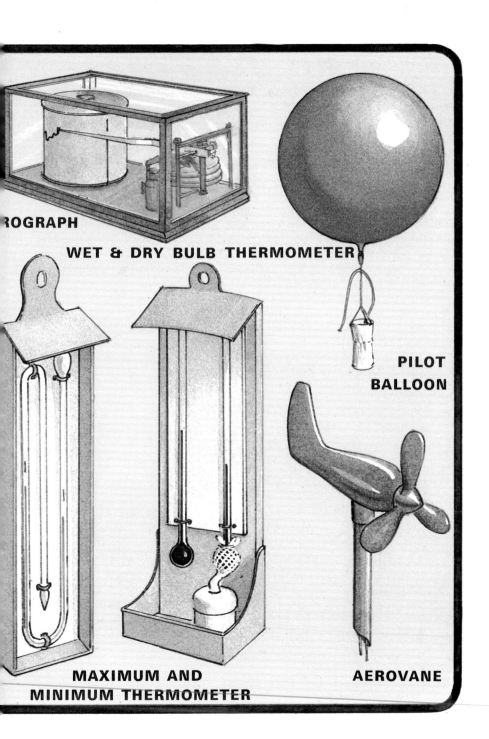

ROGRAPH

WET & DRY BULB THERMOMETER

PILOT
BALLOON

MAXIMUM AND
MINIMUM THERMOMETER

AEROVANE

HOW DOES THE BAROMETER USED IN MANY HOMES WORK?

You will often find a barometer hanging in the hall of a house or flat. It looks something like a clock, in that it has a round face, a dial with numbers and words around it, and two hands. There is no mercury in this sort of barometer.

Inside the barometer there is a small round metal box. It is completely sealed, and some of the air had been taken out of the inside. As the pressure of the atmosphere outside changes, so the sides of this box move closer together — when the outside pressure goes up — or further apart, when the outside pressure goes down.

A system of levers and little chains is fixed to this box. These are connected to one hand on the face of the dial. As the pressure changes, so the hand moves from one reading to another. It tells you whether the pressure is high or low. It also indicates something about the kind of weather you may expect to have.

The second hand on the face can be moved by you. Many people have a habit of tapping the glass early each morning. The actual measuring hand then settles at the pressure of the air, and you then set the second hand over the first, it will act as a reminder tomorrow morning when you come to read the pressure again. You can see if the pressure is higher or lower than it was.

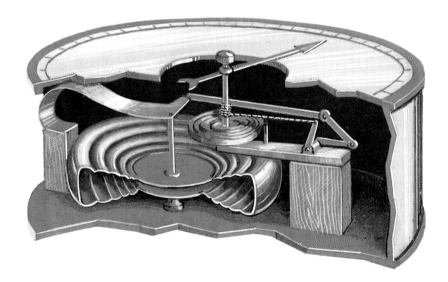

This is an aneroid barometer, which measures the pressure of the air without using mercury or other liquids. Pressure affects the delicate bellows-like round box inside, and the movements are connected to the movable pointer on the top.

WHAT IS A HYGROMETER?

A hygrometer *measures the amount of moisture* in the air. It consists of two thermometers—one called the dry bulb, and the other the wet bulb. The two thermometers are mounted upright, and side by side on a board. The dry bulb thermometer measures the actual temperature of the air. The wet-bulb thermometer gives a lower reading. This is because the bulb is covered with muslin, kept moist by some strands of cotton wick which are dipped into a small bottle of water. In this way the wet bulb thermometer is measuring the temperature of the air as if it were holding as much water vapour as it could.
Meteorologists read both thermometers at the same time, and then read some special mathematical tables to find out what the relative humidity of the air is. As a general rule, when the two temperature readings are within a degree or so of each other the relative humidity is high. When the two readings are more than one or two degrees apart, then the relative humidity is lower.

This is an anemometer. The wind blows into the cup shapes, turning a spindle. This operates a motor, and the speed is recorded on the dial.

WHAT IS AN ANEMOMETER?

This is *an instrument for measuring the speed of the wind.* It consists of three cup-shaped objects each fixed to a rod and mounted at even intervals of 120° around a central spindle. The central spindle drives a small motor and the speed of the wind is then shown on a dial which looks something like a speedometer in a car. These days you often see an anemometer on a tower crane on a building site. This is because such cranes can only work when the wind is known to be below a certain speed.

RADIOSONDE

WEATHER CENTRE

HOW DOES A THERMOMETER MEASURE TEMPERATURE?

Thermometers work because heat causes things to expand. At its simplest, a thermometer is a tube containing a liquid. If the liquid is heated, then it expands. The glass tube expands too, but nowhere near as much as the liquid does. As the liquid expands, it moves up the tube. If marks are made on the side of the tube, and they are numbered, we can make regular readings of the height reached by the liquid. This is how all thermometers work.

They are skilfully made, and use liquids such as *coloured alcohol* or *mercury.* All meteorological records are kept in *degrees Centigrade.* On this scale freezing point is 0° and boiling point is 100°. In the past some countries, including the United Kingdom, used another scale called *Fahrenheit*, but this system is no longer used officially.

WHAT ARE WEATHER STATIONS?

There are a number of different kinds of weather stations which are used for making observations and reports on the weather in various parts of the world. The best equipped are *weather observatories,* where very accurate measurements are taken, using the latest and most advanced instruments. At least every six hours, the temperature, pressure, wind speed and direction, humidity, visibility, cloud amount and cloud types and other things are observed and recorded. Then, using special codes, these stations send their records all over the world so that other meteorologists can use this information in their own work.

There are many smaller weather stations around the world. In the oceans there are special *weather ships,* and many *aircraft* send in weather reports to the countries near to where they are flying.

WHAT IS A
WEATHER SATELLITE?

These are complicated mach-
ines put into earth orbit by
man. Each one gives information on weather conditions
and related subjects. It takes
about 90 minutes for a satellite
to go once around the earth.
Satellites provide photo-
graphs of clouds and their
formations, and measure
radiation by using infra-red
film. Satellites use automatic
picture transmission. The
tracking stations on the surface of the earth can pick up
their signals as the satellites
circle the globe.

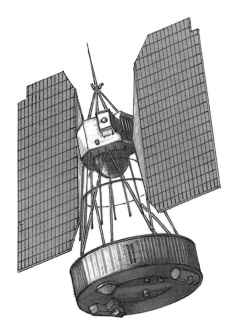

Weather satellites provide photo-
graphs of clouds and measure
radiation on infra-red type film.

HOW CAN ORDINARY PEOPLE
FORECAST THE WEATHER?

One way, of course, is to consult a barometer, and note whether the
pressure is rising or falling. Rising pressure generally is a sign of
weather improvement, and falling pressure means that the weather
is likely to get worse. Another useful piece of information is the
weather map which is usually published in newspapers, or is shown
on television. Some local authorities place a weather-map on the
notice-board at the Town Hall. Other information can be worked
out from the direction of the wind, cloud formations, visibility, and
careful note of temperature by taking readings from a thermometer
at intervals.
Some of the old weather sayings have some basis for their use, but
are as often wrong as they are right. *Red sky at night, shepherd's
delight* does not always work, but *Rain before seven, fine before
eleven* is often true in the mornings. Some people think animal
sayings have more truth in them, such as *Fast runs the ant as
mercury rises.*

HOW FAR AHEAD CAN WE FORECAST WEATHER?

When we look ahead for weather prediction, we speak of *long-range forecasts*, and they can be for anything up to about thirty days. To be reasonably accurate, weather forecasts are limited to about twenty-four hours ahead. After that, we are usually told of a further outlook, which may be less certain.

Since weather conditions can change in a matter of a few hours, long-range forecasts can only give general indications. These are now based on a period one month ahead.

WHAT ARE RAINMAKERS?

Rainmakers are commercial firms who are set up to produce rain artificially by encouraging rain-clouds to form. They have operated mainly in the United States, but not very successfully. Rain-making is really only in an experimental stage, but those experiments have shown that particles of solid carbon dioxide or dry ice dropped on to a cloud by an aircraft may produce very light rain.

Another method is to produce clouds of silver iodide—also a rain-producer—by burning its crystals in braziers in the areas where rain is needed. Whatever method is used is very expensive. It is always difficult to decide whether the rain falls as a result of the rainmakers, or whether it would have rained anyway.

A crystal of silver iodide. These crystals are burned to produce silver iodide clouds in order to make rain.

WHAT ARE WEATHER BALLOONS?

These are quite simple balloons, somewhat similar to an ordinary toy balloon, but made of much stronger material. Even a child's balloon, inflated with hydrogen, can rise to surprising heights before bursting. Many quite cheap balloons are used for weather research, and these reach heights of about 60,000 feet. More expensive balloons are used for heights up to 130,000 feet. Weather balloons carry a small, automatic radio-transmitter called a *radiosonde*. This is fitted to instruments measuring temperature, humidity and pressure. As the balloon rises it records and transmits the measurements at different heights above the earth.

Radiosondes can also be tracked by radar, and thus the speed and direction of the wind at different heights in the atmosphere can be calculated. Eventually the balloon bursts. Then the radiosonde falls back to earth on a little parachute.

WHICH COUNTRY HAS THE HOTTEST WEATHER?

Taking a yearly average, the hottest country in the world is *Ethiopia*. Records made for the years 1960-66 at *Dalol*, in the north of the country, show that the average was 34.4 °C (94 °F). Certain parts of other countries have shown higher temperatures over shorter periods of time. *Death Valley*, California, recorded 43 continuous days of temperatures over 49 °C (120 °F) from 6th July to 17th August, 1917, and *Marble Bar*, Western Australia, had temperatures of over 37.7 °C (100 °F), from 31st October to 7th April, 1924. For almost a whole year in *Wyndham*, Western Australia, the temperature exceeded 32 °C (90 °F) in 1946.

WHAT IS THE HIGHEST TEMPERATURE EVER RECORDED ON EARTH?

The world's record temperature is 58 °C (136.4 °F). This was reached at *Al'Aziziyah*, in Libya on 13th September, 1922. A near-claimant for the world's hottest place is *Greenland Ranch*, in Death Valley, California, where on 10th July 1913, the temperature recorded was 56.6 °C (134 °F). The hottest temperature ever reached in Britain was in *Tonbridge*, Kent. On 22nd July, 1868, a record 38 °C (100.5 °F) was noted.

WHAT IS THE HEAVIEST RAINFALL ON RECORD?

Cherrapunji, in Assam, India, holds the world's record for rainfall. Cherrapunji lies about 200 miles north of the Bay of Bengal, and the average rainfall is 493 inches a year. In 1860-1861, the year's total reached the incredible record of 1,041 inches. In July, 1861, the month's total reached 366 inches, an average of nearly 12 inches a day. Half the rain that falls on the place occurs in June and July, and the rest falls mainly from April to September.
In the United States, the world's fastest shower recorded was at *Opid's Camp*, in the San Gabriel Mountains, California, where 1.02 inches of rain fell in one minute on 6th April, 1926.

WHAT AND WHERE WAS THE HEAVIEST SNOWFALL?

This occurred in 1972 at *Tide Lake*, Stewart, in British Columbia, Canada, when 1,104 inches of snow fell in the year from 16th May, 1971, to 15th May, 1972. The heaviest snowfall in Britain was in 1947, when 60 inches fell during the year at *Upper Teesdale* and the *Denbighshire Hills*. At *Thompson Pass*, Alaska, on 26th-31st December, 1955, 175 inches of snow fell during a single snow-storm—a world's record for a single fall.

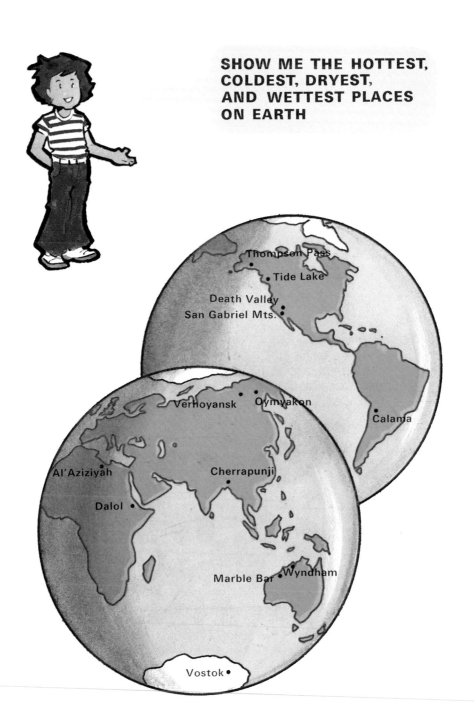

SHOW ME THE HOTTEST, COLDEST, DRYEST, AND WETTEST PLACES ON EARTH

Thompson Pass
Tide Lake
Death Valley
San Gabriel Mts.
Verhoyansk
Oymyakon
Calama
Al'Aziziyah
Cherrapunji
Dalol
Marble Bar
Wyndham
Vostok

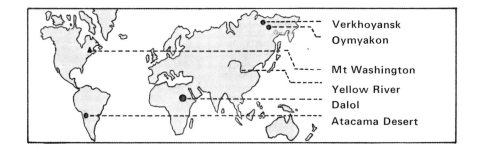

Verkhoyansk
Oymyakon

Mt Washington
Yellow River
Dalol
Atacama Desert

WHICH COUNTRY HAS THE COLDEST WEATHER?

As one would expect, the coldest country in the world is *Antarctica,* which has an annual average of −57.8 °C (−72 °F). The coldest known place there is *Vostok,* where on 24th August 1960, a temperature of −88.3 °C (−126.9 °F) was recorded. Outside Antarctica the village of *Oymyakon* in Siberia, is the coldest place on earth. During 1974, the temperature there reached a record low of −71.1 °C (−96 °F). Siberia seems to be the coldest inhabited place in the world, for another village called *Verkhoyansk,* which lies just within the Arctic Circle, has a mid-winter temperature of below −67.7 °C (−90 °F), but to compensate, the summer temperatures are sometimes as high as 33.8 °C (93 °F).

WHAT HAS BEEN THE LONGEST DROUGHT?

In the *Atacama Desert,* near Calama, Chile, no rain falls at all, and a continuous drought has been going on for at least the last 400 years !

WHERE AND WHEN WAS THE MOST DISASTROUS FLOOD?

The worst flood on record took place in August, 1931, when 3,700,000 people in China lost their lives. This was due to the overflowing of the *Hwang-Ho,* or *Yellow River,* which, because it has done so much damage in the past, has been called *China's Sorrow.* In 1887, another disastrous flood took place, when the Hwang-Ho overflowed its banks and covered 50,000 square miles of land. Three hundred villages were swept away, two million people were made homeless, and 900,000 were drowned. To make matters worse, the Hwang-Ho is not only the world's most flood-prone river, but during the summer months, the area around the Great Plain, through which it flows, is often subject to droughts.

HOW BIG ARE HAILSTONES?

In Britain, hailstones very rarely reach a size of more than half-an-inch across, although a hailstone weighing about five ounces fell in *Horsham,* Sussex, in 1958. In other countries they can be much larger. In the United States, for instance, hailstones are commonly as large as one inch across, or even more. A seven-and-a-half-inch diameter hailstone, weighing nearly a pound-and-three-quarters, fell in *Kansas* in 1970. A Viscount aircraft was battered by hailstones over India in 1959, and holes as large as five inches across were made in the wings.

Some hailstones have even been known to fall containing small live animals. One that fell in *Essen,* Germany, contained a fish one-and-a-half inches long. The up-draught of air had been so powerful that it had lifted the fish up with it, and swept it into the clouds.

WHERE WAS THE HIGHEST WIND VELOCITY RECORDED?

The greatest wind-speed recorded was at *Mount Washington,* New Hampshire, in the United States. On 12th April, 1934, a speed of 231 m.p.h. was experienced. However, in a tornado which occurred at *Wichita Falls,* Texas, the speed of the whirling wind was measured at 280 m.p.h. on 2nd April 1958. The world's windiest place is *Commonwealth Bay,* George V Coast, in Antarctica, where gales often blow at speeds of 200 m.p.h. It is sometimes difficult to make proper recordings of very high wind speeds because the instruments themselves are blown away or damaged by the tremendous force of the wind.

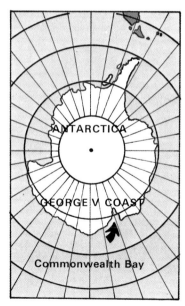

Map of Antarctica, showing the position of Commonwealth Bay.

DO YOU KNOW . . .

Where is the longest railway bridge?

What are the temperate zones?

Who invented computers?

Which is the biggest waterfall?

What sort of animal is Man?

Which plant has the largest flower?

How do we measure heat?

Who discovered the Pacific Ocean?

When did the aircraft industry begin?

Which is the fastest train in the world?

Where is the Valley of Ten Thousand Smokes?

What was Atlantis?

Who was Professor Junkers?

How did civilisation begin?

What is a diurnal animal?

*You will find the answers to these, and
hundreds of other questions in pages full
of fascinating facts, if you begin collecting
all the titles in the QUIZZER BOOK series!*

Printed in Spain   Depósito legal B. 26.618-1975   Printer industria gráfica, sa
Tuset, 19   Barcelona   Sant Vicenç dels Horts   1975
Colour Separations by Newsele, Milán